MAKE YOUR DREAM COME TRUE!

FLORENCIA MENNA

Ordering Information:

Prime Seven Media
518 Landmann St.
Tomah City, WI 54660

Printed in the United States of America

Dedication

This book is dedicated to my mother, Cristina Nanzi, who always supported me in all my crazy things since I was little.

To my dad, Nicholas Menna that, although he's not with us anymore, I know he'd be very proud of his daughter because, honestly, if I had not inherited his determination and drive to achieve what he intended, I would have not have gotten where I find myself now. When something got into his head, there was nothing or no one to stop him until he made it.

And, at last, but not less important, to my English teacher Jorge Rodriguez, because without his method for teaching the language, today I could not speak nor would I get by here in England as I do now. So my message to him is:

Thanks, teacher! And let *The Music Duende's music* return! (*)

(*) Radio program broadcast by FM de Sol Benito Juárez, during the years 1980 to 1987 and 1989 to 1995.

Author's Biography

From Benito Juárez to Bedford

I was born on December 7, 1976, in Benito Juárez, Buenos Aires, Argentina. Sagittarius with all the marks!

I went to elementary school at the Immaculate Conception School and part of high school at the Pedro Díaz Pumará Institute (IPDP) and then, as I already knew I wanted to study Economics, I finished the last two years of high school at the National School of Commerce Dr. Benito Juárez.

I completed my higher studies at the National University of the Center of the Province of Buenos Aires (UNCPBA) of Tandil, Buenos Aires, Argentina, where I also studied three years of International Relations, a career that, as I told in one of the chapters of this book, I couldn't finish. Back in Benito Juárez, I continued with a technical degree in SME Business Administration, which later helped me for my business "Aromas de Flor", which I had for 12 years.

As you will read later, I studied the British English language since I was a little child and, when I moved back to Tandil, I also studied Italian at Dante Alighieri, since my job required it. It is also the native language of my father and my grandparents on both sides, with which I was familiar since I was a child. In other words, you could say that I am a pure Italian descendant!

After going through several jobs and situations in life that were quite unfortunate, I decided to leave my job in the Board of Italians, sell my business to fulfill my dream and move to England, where I now live since August 2018. Here, I found my place, Bedford, in Bedfordshire County, where I settled a year ago. I am working for the No. 1 company in the world in the area of robotics, but I always leave some time to devote myself to what I like, which is to help people through Reiki and Life Coaching in which I got certified here in England.

On my days off, I allow myself to go for walks or enjoy long walks by the river and park area of this city and practice one of my hobbies, which is taking pictures, some of which you will see in this book.

More information about the author at: www.descubretupropialuz.com

Contact links with Florencia Menna

Website:

www.florenciamennacoach.com

Instagram:

https://www.facebook.com/mennaflor

Facebook:

https://www.facebook.com/mennaflor

E-mail:

floraromadeflor@gmail.com

YouTube:

https://www.youtube.com/channel/UCBCs6bFBOL-vWmztTomxJZg

LinkedIn:

https://www.linkedin.com/in/florencia-menna-054a3916a/

Introduction

Dear reader: if you are looking in this book to know my personal story with all its details, it is likely that you will find some of that, yes, but that is not only what I am telling here.

Now, if you have a dream and so far you have not been able to carry it out -for whatever the reason- I want you to know that you are in the right place and, as you read these pages, you will not only feel identified with my story, but also motivated to work and carry out your own experience.

What I want with my book is to inspire you so that you too can fulfill your dream, whatever it may be, and it doesn't necessarily have to be moving to another country, no! Look inside yourself for the biggest wish you've had since you were little, what you liked to do so much or wanted to be when you grew up, do you remember? Well, that same one!

The path to achieve it will not be easy, but if every day you do part a little bit and, above all, trust in your own power, I promise you that very soon you will make it happen!

And now you will ask yourself: and how do I do it?
Very simple: work on it!

And how do I work in my dream if I don't know what I want?

What I propose, at this precise moment when you are reading this book, is that you ask yourself the following: Are you happy? Are you doing what you really want to do? Do you feel that you are where you would like to be?

If some of these questions generated a negative answer, then search within yourself what would be your ideal situation, and when you have it very clear, go for it!

Do not abandon or put aside your dream, demoralized by what others tell you: they have not been able to fulfill their own and therefore they do not care if you fulfill yours. Also, don't let the situation you find yourself in (economy, family, the place where you live, etc.) stop you from materializing them.

If you really want it, then do it!

If you like to paint, paint! It may not be a work of art like those of the great artists of history, but who will take away the pride of having your own painting?

If you like to sing, sing! Do you think you are not good? Take classes!

Do you think that the great musicians we know were born singing as they later did? No! They worked on their voice to find the right tone, as did the musicians for their bands.

Did you adore ballet as a child? I insist, take classes! You may not be presenting at the Colón Theater, but your body will once again feel that sensation of floating in the air with each movement.

What I mean is that there is no age, time, money, style or excuse that you want to put out for not doing it. Today the options are many, varied and accessible to everyone, so don't think twice and get to work!

If you don't do it now, when do you plan to do it? The time is now, do it!

Enjoy my book!

Index

Chapter 1

What do you want to do when you grow up?

Travel to London! Is what I always answered. And why did I say this? Because I, since I was little, since I started studying English at the age of seven, I was very clear that what I wanted was to travel and live in London. I loved the fog, the red double-decker buses, the red phone booths, the old black cabs, the typical English way of speaking, the people, and their elegance. I loved to drink tea. My mom always had porcelain English at home, and I loved those tea sets in fact I used one of those cups to drink some when I came from school, something that my classmates did not do because they were taking milk as most ordinary children ... and I say "ordinary" because I never I considered myself that way, feeling that there was something different, don't know why, I always thought it was due to me being born with a heart defect and having to have surgery before I was even 2 years old; I was very close to death, and then my parents raised and protected me as a 'hothouse flower" (they always said that to me), and if we add that I was a daughter of older parents... That'd be why I was raised differently. I was a rather quiet girl, shy, but very polite and dedicate to my studies.

But going back to what I wanted to do when I grew up...

How did I prepare for that? Between seven and eleven years old I had already decided this: I'd finish studying high school and would study business administration at the university (I ended up changing majors and I chose the commercial orientation on the third year), and once I graduated, I would go to live in London and establish my company there!

By that time, the company that I dreamed to have would be about fashion and I even had the name and logo design! It would be called "Florence's Vogue".

What did I do? I started preparing myself, first of all, as previously mentioned, I started studying British English not the American, as most people usually learn. First, I started with a teacher, then, over time, I saw that I was not making progress in content. I realized this talking with others kids who were with other private teachers and had other books, knew other words, using other learning systems. I talked about it with Mom and, even though we were sad to leave my teacher because she was very good, she decided to send me with other teacher, to whom I am eternally grateful. I remember when I first entered the study room: I was surprised because it had what they call a "language laboratory" with booths and headphones, very different from what I was used to. We put strong emphasis on phonetics, which is what nowadays I use to pronounce as the words as well as I do, which is rather surprising to locals.

My teacher had all the looks of a gentleman then, and that excited me even more because he really looked like an English gentleman.

A few years after starting studying with him, he won a contest with a monograph on the Beatles on the Badía television program and traveled to London. Imagine how I felt! Euphoric! Because I felt that, through him, I was fulfilling my dream of traveling to London. I was very excited! I remember that he brought me a postcard from London and I was super anxious to hear how everything was there, although the truth is that he was not very expressive, so he did not say much, but we listened very attentively to how little he told us and we stayed very excited that someday we would know those places.

I enjoyed through him! It was the first experience that someone I knew traveled to London.

Let's agree that, at this time, I am speaking of the years 1985 to 1987, it was not like nowadays, and I do not speak of this year 2020 in particular. Let's say that a few years ago it became more accessible for everyone to travel. At that time, practically very few people traveled, not only because of the costs, but because it was not something that simple or common to do or accessible for everyone, so that was my first experience with someone who traveled to "my beloved" London.

So, I was preparing, polishing more and more the language, the pronunciation. I was always formal when dressing; I always tried to be aware of the news from there. For example, New Year came and I celebrated at 8pm in Argentina, because I knew that in England it was midnight, and things like that. For the World Cup, I obviously was rooting for Argentina, but when England played with teams from other nations, I rooted for them! But if they played against Italy I had to cheer Italy because Dad would get angry with me!

On the other hand, I felt a contradiction or, better said, a feeling of guilt, because my brother was in the Malvinas, more precisely in Rio Grande and, although I was five years old at that time, I remember my mother crying because she had no news about him. And I didn't understand much, but I do remember that in kindergarten there was a poster and I told them, proudly, that my brother was there. I remember that teachers looked at me with sad faces and I didn't quite understand why they looked at me like that... Over the years I understood, of course! And then it made things hard; on the one hand, there was this desire to know and live in England with all that it entailed, and another thing was that feeling of wronging my brother (thankfully he returned safely shortly after), and I lived with this until a few days before to come to live here, just in the days my brother among other partners received an acknowledgment; so, he told them about my plans, and It was then that one of them told me that I shouldn't feel bad for them, that I was very young at that time (1982) and I didn't have to carry a feeling that did not belong to me. And he added, "I was also in England a few years ago and not for that was I not going to meet the place, I also have friends there, so be calm, go live and enjoy your new life there without any guilt!"

Those words comforted me so much because, until that moment, it was like I needed that kind of "permission" from them to be able to face what was coming to me.

On the other hand, there was another great motive involved in this great dream. And the thing is that I, in those years (1985-1987), was a fan of the British duo Pet Shop Boys and I confess that, like every teenage in love with her idol, I was a fan of Neil, the singer. When I was eleven years old I told my classmates in school that when I finished studying, I'd go to live to London, establish my company and I would marry him! Obviously my classmates laughed and even made fun of that. Of course, that came to nothing, but that's teenage dreams, as I said, we all had them...

I was always aware of everything they did, although not much information or material from them reached Argentina. I had a hard time getting their cassettes. Now living in England, I realize that they never stopped, they always were there, and continually put out material that never arrived there (Argentina). So, as I could, I'd get cassettes recorded or would get someone else to record them for me and, well, when finally a new one arrived to the record store it was a joy, but the truth is that it was rather expensive. From time to time there'd be a poster in the magazine 13/20 and in Smash Hits (that's still publishing here).

So, as I was saying, in my own way I was trying to maintain a sort of "English culture", and at eleven I was reading Shakespeare (my favorites, *Hamlet* and *Henry V*) as a way to do it.

What I wanted at that time was to start saving money to buy the ticket, whose value I already knew, something like 1,100 (I do not remember exactly at that time what currency we had, I do not know if they were southern or Argentine peso, I do not know), and my brother gave me the first five dollars to start (although I knew their currency was the pound).

Eventually, I was collecting some money I received for birthdays or for other reasons, in short, what I was given by my family, and I bought ten sterling pounds! I had them until I came to live here, then I had to change them because although the country is very traditional and don't change anything, just as I was to come, they changed their currency! Then those were no longer useful, so I had to exchange them at the Bank of London where, of course, they received them and gave me the same value on a new note. The bank teller was very surprised and happy to see a bill from that era! But the anecdotal thing was to keep those ten pounds -which I adored- for thirty years. They were practically nothing compared to the amount I needed for the plane ticket, but for me, it was like a very advanced step that I had to take to be able to get it.

Now with time I see it and think: how crazy that was!

As I told you, my classmates laughed at me and my ideas. Those closest to me used to tell me: "Yeah right, you're going to fall in love with a singer!", "Sure, you're going to go to London!" And things like that. They told me I was very fanciful, but I was very conscious and determined about what I wanted. I was always very organized in all my stuff, so I had confidence in myself that I was going to get there, it was my goal and nothing they said was going to stop me.

I continued studying English until I finished high school. Then, I went to study in another city, Tandil, and at the university we had English courses, so I keep on studying with the language, but no on private classes.

When I began to study was when things started to change…

I was no longer so eager about my dream; I had grown up, I was 17 and obviously I was not in the same mindset anymore, but of course, I was always steady on the dream of at least going just to know London. That was always on my mind and it was my goal, and I would not change it for the world!

What happens is that one does not realize at first, but what was changing were the scenarios, the people around me and who I was getting to know, the situations, well, LIFE itself!

Chapter 2

Thirty years is nothing

That's right! Because thirty years did pass, and now I think about it and say: wow, thirty years! And there are others who can tell me: "And did it take you thirty years to fulfill your dream?" No! It is that it-was-hard, it's that this was not the moment but, by destiny, it had to be. Then these thirty years were not in vain nor wasted.

No, quite the opposite! I had to go through those years in order to achieve my goal of being here today, living in England.

They were thirty hard years because many things happened in the middle. As I said in the previous chapter, life takes you elsewhere, by other ways, you know people you whom might think in that moment that you should not have ever known, but in reality everything is inside of one divine plan, to put it in words; getting to know these people, living in other places and then being able to be where and with whom you should really be. Everything leads you to being able to continue towards your goal. It is not simple to be aware of this! But a time already spent is when you say, 'Oh, it was for this reason! ". And you feel comforted to have gone through them when you see the results obtained.

Everything that I started in my youth, little by little, faded, that interest, that drive that I had as the only objective of my life: to finish my degree and go to London.

I could not finish my studies because, in the middle, my dad got sick and I had to return from where I was studying because we could not continue to pay for the place where I was living. Things already changed there, I went back to my hometown, to Benito Juarez. Before going to study, one of the projects was to enter the Student Deliberative Council, because it was precisely about the creation of a "Casa Juarez" in Tandil, where students could reside on, paying by small installments or something like that, but, well, the idea was that it could be done. At that time, it was not achieved, but many years later it was, and I was satisfied, because one of my projects (although its origin was never acknowledged) had finally been fulfilled, and many young students would benefit from this. For me it was too late.

Then, I started working on a commission to create a university in Benito Juarez, I participated in the commission, the project took place and I, years after it's founded, I enrolled in one of the programs they offered. By then, I was increasingly diverted from fulfilling my dream of moving to London. At that time, my only objective was how to get out of that city and return to Tandil, which was where my maternal family always was, my mother was actually born there. I felt that I could not go on living in Benito Juárez, and despite having been born there, I did not belong to that place.

In those years, (since then the city has changed a lot), there weren't many jobs offers or opportunities if you stayed there. It was either going to work or studying elsewhere, because if you stayed there was very little to do.

So my first job was running a stand and, well, I was living a life that was not the one I wanted at all, but we had to continue... It was from 1998 to 2003 that we finally sold the house and moved with mom to Tandil. In 1999, my sister passed away due to an aneurysm, and that took us by such a surprise that even to this day I'm still unable to understand how I could talk to her in the afternoon and on the evening I was telling my brother in law that she was unresponsive, went to emergencies and were told about her death, something unexpected and incomprehensible...

In 2001 my father, who had been on dialysis for years, died; his body no longer resisted the treatment. This coincided with the end of my college career, for which, as you could imagine, I wasn't in a spirit to celebrate.

But going back to those years, for me they were terrible because I was in a place where I did not want to be, doing what I did not want to do, having gone through two terrible losses, and I saw that every time I was turning off more and more, all that energy, that euphoria, that desire to live, to do, to fight, little by little, they were disappearing. I wasn't me anymore. I wasn't truly Florencia, I was not that enthusiastic Sagittarius that I'd always been... there was not much to do and I felt more and more stagnant. But I continued doing it because, well, I was with my mother and I had to do things the same, I had to work, I had to continue the same way, but it was not what I wanted the most. Later, I went to work as a telephone operator in a taxi service, but that was not my goal either. I started over again on English with another teacher, it was just to talk, to practice, but it was not the same; I didn't have enough money to go back to private classes.

Those were difficult years for me, because I really felt the suffocated and stagnant by being there, there was no way to get rid of them, I wanted to leave, I wanted to return to Tandil and I didn't know if it would be to continue my studies, but at least to do something else, I knew that somewhere else I could get another kind of job and have more opportunities.

What I got over those years was that, over time and after a lot of internal work, I understood and accepted the true reason for having been born in Benito Juarez and not in another place, as I, more than once, raised that question. I always asked myself that for many years, and I found the reason: it had to be like that, I had to be born there, I had to meet the people I met there, wonderful people who write to me today to congratulate me on my strength and courage (they say) for having made the decision to leave everything and go for my dream, and they also show me their affection and also how with my story, I have motivated many people to face their dreams, and that is the truth that fills my soul. Most people say, "I knew you since little, I always saw you holding your mom or dad's hand" and that's very nice, that's very important and something I value, and today I realize that it in fact those people are the ones who are really worth it.

In Tandil, actually, I never managed to be recognized for anything, that is, I was one more person who lived there. On the other hand, in Juarez everyone knew who I was, whose daughter I was, in short, I had a defined personality, in the sense that you feel appreciated, that is what I mean, that they know you, that you feel that YOU ARE SOMEONE. I did a lot in Tandil and I was never taken into account or valued, that is what I felt.

When we finally sold the house in 2003 and moved to Tandil with my mom, it seemed as I was in heaven, I finally got what I wanted, but after a few months passed it ended up not being as such, "not all that shines is gold" they said to me once, and so it was. It seemed that everything showed great potential but it was not like that, it was also difficult to get a job -we are talking about 2003, after the great crisis of 2001- so I also worked in what I could... at the beginning I was working on my brother's business, later I went to clean floors in a bookstore in the morning, again as telephone operator in a taxi service, whatever came up, that is, it was not my objective, I was still in the same situation, the only thing that had changed was the location but it was still not me, still not Florencia, as I knew myself. But I couldn't find myself, nor recognize myself...

It took me three years until I said to my mother: "Look, I want to do something." I had some savings and I proposed to her: "if you help me, I can create a business." And she gladly accepted. And so Aromas de Flor was made, which I owned for twelve years, and it was like my own child to me. I made soaps and handmade cosmetics, I had my own brand and I started it in the living room of the first house we had when we moved; later, in the house that we have to this day, I modified the garage and made it a sales place.

I loved making the products because I really put passion into it. I love scents, in fact, I chose that item because I really liked buying those kinds of products, so I knew I was choosing something that I enjoyed doing.

Over the years, *Aromas de Flor* did not grow, that feeling of stagnation returned, and even though it sold well it did not evolve, it was always at the same level, I wanted to go out to sell other locations, to other provinces and why not, to even export! But there was no way, and I say there was no way because there were no resources, plus I did everything myself, and I didn't have much help either. Some close friends told me: "you should have a partner", but I didn't want to. It's that I did not feel that that was the problem, but that it was something else that still did not define well what it was.

It was twelve years of having the business and I saw that It couldn't go much longer, they told me, my brother told me: "look, you will have to leave that because it is not going anywhere", and I refused to see reality, and it was the only thing I had of my own. At that point, the trip to London or England was completely forgotten, practically buried, as if I had never even had that idea in my head once.

During the crisis of the business and a bad relationship I also had, in the midst of all that I said to myself: "this so cannot go on...

Something has to change". So I made the decision to go live in the closest England could be to me, which was the south. I planned everything, I contacted people from there, they all motivated me to go because there was work there, in short, when I am about to do it because I had already decided, I participate in a Family Constellations workshop, and the constellator, Trixie Moura asks me: "Do you really want to go because you really like it there and you want to do it, or because you want to escape from your current situation?" And there I thought about it and that question clicks with me, and I said, "I think the latter" and then she said, "Wherever you go if you do not change yourself, you are going to carry that baggage with you". In other words, in Juarez, in Tandil, and I was going to feel the same in the south, or worse because I was going to be more alone.

So I gave up on that decision and continued with the business a little longer, always turning it around with innovations, with different things to renew it.

Participating with *Aromas de Flor* on Holistic Expo 2015

Chapter 3

The first signs

As I was telling you, I came with a business that was not progressing, with my personal life that had not come to fruition either, I had had a terrible experience, seven months after saying: "why did I meet this guy?", And then, as I said later, over time you realize that I had to know certain people to be where I am.

I felt that for me everything was lost... I don't know if it was lost, but it seemed that there was no way out, and if there was, I couldn't find it. In that period of time my cousin traveled to London and there, instead of accompanying this moment -not that I was not happy for him-, I felt hurt, because there were more people who were already starting to go and I still wasn't able to, and I thought that I'd never would. The following year, my brother traveled with the family and, well, the same empty feeling, happy for them, of course, because when they came back they told me that when they were there they saw everything that I always told them I wanted to see, and then it was like they lived it and enjoyed it through my life stories. In short, it seemed that somehow I was there with them, but I was not the one who was there.

I admit that those trips affected me, they bothered me, because I said and I came to think, just a year before my first trip, the following (through tears and very disappointed in myself and the life I had at that time) : "I'm going to die and I'm never going to see London." Those were my words, and today I repeat them and I feel again that anguish that I felt when pronouncing them. Even today there are moments that, if not because I see certain details from here, I don't truly realize that I am really living here, and I am saying it and I get excited again. But I really felt that way, that I was never going to be able to travel because there was no way to get the resources, everything was wrong, there was already an economic crisis, and as I say, business was not going well, my other job was getting worse. (I represented a patronage of Italians in Tandil, Buenos Aires, it was a service that was provided for which people were not charged anything, and for which I received a very low income, which was not enough for me at all). It was taking time; in fact I even used up space in my house for something that I saw that there was no point in continuing to do. I did that for nine years, I helped many people, many got citizenship and pensions because of my services, but personally, let's say, my only benefit was seeing people happy or satisfied with their procedure being done, of course, but that did not make me feel accomplished on a personal level, there would be no growth in future to say: step to the next level which is, to put an example, working for a consulate or embassy, no, that'd never happen, not at all, I was just continuing to do paperwork for years, and in fact, nine years was enough time to do it, on top of being parallel to my business.

I felt very tired and emotionally worn out, until February 2015, if I have to say it, I don't remember how it came about, that is, how I received the invitation. I honestly don't remember that detail exactly, but they invited me to a cultural tour to Mar del Plata to visit the Museum of the Sea and the House of the Bridge of the architect Amancio Williams. In the Museum of the Sea, among all the exhibits of different artists of modern art, one of the Argentine artists Diana Aisenberg drew my attention, she presented large green slates on which very specific questions were written; one of them was "What is your dream?" And I had to think about it at that moment because it had been completely erased from my memory! There was no longer the desire to go to live in England. When I read that question and I ask myself: "What is my dream?" I stop for a few moments to think and I answer: "well, actually, the dream I always had was to go live in London." So I wrote that on the board. And believe me that was the first sign I had: when I left it on a blackboard with my own handwriting, it was as if stopped cogs started running again and they were just missing some oil to function again. And that's how, little by little, that longing began to sink again.

And that day was very nice, we had a great time with the group that shared that cultural tour, the coordinator was María Menegazzo, who was delightful, and excellent in everything about art. It could be said that that day was the beginning of the countdown to my journey.

Anyway, prior to this -I'm going back a bit-, amid the tremendous crisis that I had, I was suggested a Reiki course, and I said no, that I didn't know if I'd like it or could come to do Reiki to others, but I did like taking sessions.

But someone convinced me and told me: "try to just do the first level, it will be good for you, you'll see."

I ended up doing the three levels in a matter of two years, and it really changed me a lot, also accompanied by Family Constellations and Alejandro Gatti, who helped me a lot to see things from another point of view on a more psychological level. Those two therapies helped me a lot and were the starting motor to begin to, little by little, get out of the agony I felt.

To want to evolve, to be better, to want to go back to being who I was, because I didn't recognize myself, I was totally unknown to me, and doing the Reiki courses helped me a lot as well. So once completed the three levels, I built an office in my house and started helping many people; it was amazing really. They were really grateful people, I had patients with very difficult problems, seeing how they came and how they evolved in their end, on their healing, and everything worked out, let's say, by my hands, that gave me a lot of strength and I got the confidence back in me same that I had lost it. I had very complex cases, but the one I remember the most was a man with terminal cancer who came to see me to "prepare" himself for his final stage; for me that was a huge challenge but I took it with love and respect, not only could he travel to Buenos Aires to face a new surgery, but he also came out well, three months later he came to see me very grateful, and he even looked much better than that day when he first entered my office. A few years passed when I found out that he'd finally left us, but, as they told me, in great peace.

I started doing meditation workshops on Saturdays, and people were leaving very happy and grateful because they discovered internal things that maybe they did not realize or did not see it until they surfaced through meditation.

And everything was like that, I repeat: the artist's thing was in February 2015... And I continued with all those jobs and I had already started an evolution on a personal level. Little by little, I began to get out of that nebula in which I found myself more and more to reach the light, but I still could not find a concrete way out to reconnect with myself, that was still difficult for me and I still had to reach it. There was still a lot to do, even though Reiki and meditations had helped me a lot. But I still had to find the Florencia that I knew so well, the determined, the authentic, enthusiastic and full of energy. So I had to keep working on that.

February 2015 – writing on the "magic blackboard"

Chapter 4

I finally woke up

October 2015. It was at night, I was about to go to bed; like every day, I turned on the radio to hear some music, I liked to keep it low to sleep, which I no longer do, but at that time I used to. I tuned in a station and, after listening to several songs, suddenly one starts playing, of all the ones I'd been listening at that moment, none had captured me like that one did, it was something that went directly into heart, soul, I don't know, but it deeply moved me. It was incredibly beautiful, and the most exciting thing was hearing at the end the applause and ovation of the audience towards those musicians. I didn't know who they were, or what that song was called, so I remembered that on my cell phone I had the application to search for songs; I do it and the result was that the song was called Sebastian and the band Steve Harley and Cockney Rebel. It was new to me, never in my life had I heard their name nor them singing, and the song, I tell you, was incredible. I looked for the video on YouTube, and with the images and everything it was even more exciting, and the singer was an English man, as I always dreamed of in those moments of mine when I went to English class when I was little, and I said: "who is he? Who are they? Why do they get me?" There I started to looking for information and downloaded the song in my phone.

That ended there. Some time passed, specifically two months, and in December, I had forgotten that I had saved the song on my cell phone. One afternoon I was sunbathing on the patio of my house (which did not have much time or space to do it because it was surrounded by houses and trees, so the time in the sun was minimal), I put on the headphones listening to the playlists that I had recorded on my cell phone, and at that moment I saw the clouds pass, just observing them and trying to make a shape of the strange forms they acquire, and meditate on the magnitude and infinitude of the sky, and suddenly that song appears again, *Sebastian*! And it kept playing and playing…. And when the violin solo began, tears welled up in my eyes and I went off to mourn with as much feeling as a child does, and it was like it came from inside myself, it went through me like a breath all the darkness stuck inside me all those years… all that anguish, bad, and ugly situations that had happened, as if everything went out, it was a feeling of relief, a tremendous relief, in fact, it was as if I came back to life, as if it had been without being able to breathe during all that time and suddenly they had helped me to breathe again. That was the feeling I had, it was incredible, it was a feeling that I can try to explain but it'd be difficult to express how I felt. That was what I felt with that song. And it was there, in that instant, between tears, crying hopelessly, that I ask myself: "what am I doing here?" Because really there was no reason, nothing satisfied me, I couldn't find anything that made sense to living there, in that incredibly bland way, to say. And then I ask myself, forgetting that I had been in front of that board few months ago, in the museum: "What had I wanted to do since I was little?" And there among excited sobs, the answer comes in immediately to my mind: "travel and live in London!" And that was the kick-off, that was the awakening that I had to go back to focus on the goal that always had, but that life situations, people I'd met, the environment, jobs that I'd had made me forget, made it so my memory of that I've wished for so many years truly disappeared.

So, I decided to find out more about that band, who they were, learn more songs, and do you know what one of them is called? *El Faro*! (You'll see in a few chapters why I mention this). I even wanted contact them, looking at the videos over and over and over again and got excited every time I saw them, pulling all-nighters (it was 4 am and I was still watching their videos), and there I thought: "I have to go see these people", I found out that they were performing in April 2016 in England (it's an English band in fact). At that time, I did not have any money, or anything, no possible way to travel, there was no way to do it, and I said, "I do not know how I'll do, but I'm going to be there!". And that was the next goal I set for myself, "I have to be there." And what was I going to get from it? Achieving the dream of my life, that is what it was going to get, and they were the road to that, they had been a big "alarm clock" for me a huge sign that told me to see the light through the song and rediscover what I truly wanted to do.

If you want you can see the video with the song *Sebastian* by
Steve Harley & Cockney Rebel that I heard and saw for the first time

Chapter 5

The three most intense months of my life

And why do I say this? Because from that day I proposed myself that I had to be there to see to the band live, and that obviously I had no idea how to get the resources to do so, in fact, I didn't even have a passport! Or, better said, I had it, but it was expired, because since I always had the idea of traveling I'd gotten my passport, and got it ready, but now that I needed it, I didn't have it.

So I began to find ways to communicate with them in some way and tell my story, what had happened because of their song, I wanted them to know what their music had achieved. Then I found a website and an official group on Facebook and I saw the days and weeks pass but in this group there was no movement, it was paralyzed.

There I was elated, excited because I had returned to life, again feeling the desire to live, to do things, to learn.

I had been baffled about this song, their music, their voices, the band itself; I was as excited as a teenager, and again returned to feel like in my teens. Therefore, I decided on my own to create a group on Facebook of Steve Harley and Cockney Rebel Friends, I posted it out and British people began to appear and they were being added to the group. There were originally twelve of us; one was from Italy, most of them from England, and one from France. When I met them (obviously later on) I asked them: "What did you guys think of me?", because I would think: "Who is this girl from the other end of the world, who creates a group of a band that she has just found out about?" They came along with the band since its inception, for more than 40 years, and I had just discovered them, it was all so crazy!

So, because I was so excited, I started looking for photos, videos, it was all the time, all the time posting, and since I had all this free time... I was continuously posting information, material, images that many of them had never really seen. The members of the group I had created did not know each other. They went to concerts, but each one on their own, there was no link between them except for some who entered later.

To this day this group, which of course I still keep, has more than 500 members worldwide, and they were and are very grateful and fascinated with me, and they told me so when they showed up for the first time, because what was curious to them was knowing where I got the information, the videos, the photos, how I had all that and, on the other hand, what they were grateful for was that thanks to the fact that I had created that virtual group I had brought them together, after 40 years of following the band, and it had made them feel like they went back in time to that 70's when they started playing. Imagine what that meant to me!

So the group grew and grew, and as I said, today we are at exactly 554 members; Of course, everything is spoken in English, and I was always valued and respected, there were never any questions of any kind, on the contrary, they were always very happy and grateful that I created that group. At the same time, I got an e-mail and contacted the band's contact office.

I had already bought the ticket for the concert, and of course I still didn't know if I could travel because I didn't have the money, but I bought it anyway, that is, I had it, and it was as if it were already the "ticket" for that trip.

When I contacted the agency or office, I introduce myself and tell them that I already have the ticket and that I planned to go in April. Obviously, what I omitted to say was that I didn't have the money for the plane ticket yet.

One of those sleepless nights, I wrote a letter to the singer telling the story of what happened to me with that song, what I felt, what I experienced, and all this I started to build and was generated through of the song. So, with my email and the members of the group, there was quite a move there in England: look at this girl, look at what she's building from the other side of the world!

At the same time, I started to meditate because the new year (2016) had started, and I had spent two months to do all that, and on New Year I started a meditation which also came strangely to my email because I did not remember being subscribed Nor have I heard about it before, it was about Chamalu, a shaman from Bolivia with a lot of wisdom and teachings who offered the possibility of meditating together with him and, on this occasion, because it was the beginning of a new year, he proposed a very special meditation that lasted 12 days, representing 12 months of the year, in which you had to place your intention for each one of them.

It was a guided meditation and had to make visualization, and in the first three days I couldn't concentrate nor saw anything, I did it, I relaxed, yes, but nothing more. When the 4th arrived, representing the month of April, I felt through this meditation as if I was rising and transported to another place, as if I left behind the place where I was physically to pass into an ethereal body. I usually did it in my room sitting on the bed, and at that moment it felt like a blast of air that transported me to another place, and took me to a cliff surrounded by green meadows and the sea below, that is, I was up on the cliffs and saw the beach below, in the distance, and to my right where the cliff ended, there was a lighthouse. To me, lighthouses had always called my attention, It caused a feeling of love and sadness at the same time, never knew what for, but I always loved them, they attracted me, I know... I always had this fascination with them, I didn't know too many, but with the few that I saw I felt that.

And I was there, sitting in that meadow, in this visualization that I was doing through meditation, but that for me at that moment was very real, and I was there in that place, and in a moment a person appeared, a tall man, with blond curly hair dressed in a typical English look, -the name of Jefferson came to my mind-, I smiled, not saying a word, he just smiles at me and gives me a smile and with it transmits me a tremendous peace, and reaching forth his hand, his gaze and through his thoughts I felt as if he were saying to me: "I was waiting for you." And at that moment, once again I burst into tears, because I always had the thought of that in reality my life was in another place or that maybe in another life I had belonged to this place and that's why I could not realize anything about where I was, because that was really where everything had to happen. So it was an incomparable and indescribable feeling, my heart seemed like it was going to explode. It was all very exciting and I was convinced of that's how it'd be. I returned to my present state, that is, to meditation, to the guide who was making me return, and I go back to my room and there I burst into tears once more, I couldn't believe what had happened to me.

The following days, I anxiously waited for the moment of meditation, I returned to transport myself to that place and that man who always appeared, sat next to me with his smile transmitting a calm, a peace, as if everything was going to be fine, that what I was planning to do was fine, that I should do that trip.

At that time, a week or so, after all this, I had met a client of my business who told me: "Look, I'm doing akashic records, I can read yours whenever you want" It seemed that everything was planned for me to do so, because what had happened with the song and with the meditation, and now this girl who proposed that to me, were new signals that they were sending me that something was brewing, something beyond a simple trip. There must be something else...

So, I accepted the invitation and went. She did not know anything about all what I was going through, I did not comment on anything at all, indeed, she just knew me. And starting the reading of records, it was shown that I was going to make a trip to one place where there are castles and is very old, where there are forests, mountains, but mostly it showed it as a very old place, and it appeared on her visualization, or rather, what the Guides showed her, and through her they transmitted to me, it was like uffff!, I say it and it still gives me such a special feeling that it gives me goose bumps. She tells me: "I see a lighthouse," and I had never told her about the lighthouse, there was no way for her to know that. And she continues: " a lighthouse appears , and you, in another life you were in this very old place where there are very green meadows, and you were with a person, with a man, you were fine, as in a couple, but something happened and you decided go jump from that lighthouse. "Imagine. I was stunned because, I repeat, my emotions when I saw the lighthouses were of admiration, but they also generated sadness in me, and with what she was telling me I could find the reason for that feeling. I was still intrigued by this topic, and she tells me: "and that person saved you, you didn't manage to throw yourself away and that person is like he's waiting there for you now." And there, well, the summum because I repeat, I never mentioned anything to her at all about my visualization or anything, that is, something was actually there, obviously the Guides were really there next to me and they were guiding me and confirming that I should make that trip at any cost. So it motivated me even more to work on getting the ticket and actually doing it!

I had always had the feeling, apart from, of course, traveling to England, that I wanted to see Ireland, I always said: "I don't want to die without first seeing the green Irish meadows", that was my catchphrase. But I saw Ireland as an even further place, much less feasible than going to England, it was like a parallel dream that I had never put much energy into, it was a newer dream if you like, from not so long ago; I had always said only that, that it attracted me. I had the idea with England since I was a girl that I had lived there, that in my other life I had been there, my idea, my feeling was that I should "return" to England although I had never been in my life -at least not in my current life- evidently in another life it seems that I was.

With Ireland what happens to me —and happened to me at that moment after that reading and that I always said I wanted to know— it's as if my soul had been there, and in a certain way belonged to that place —to explain it in an understandable way to make my point-, but it is what I felt and that different things transmitted to me more and more.

I definitely decided to set up the trip and go to the recital, which was on April 23, 2016, I left Argentina on the 21st and arrived on the 22nd, and the next day after the recital I was going to Ireland. It was a whirlwind trip, because it meant putting everything together, and I still didn't have the resources, that's why I called this chapter the-three-most-intense-months-of-my-life, because in that short time I achieved what it took me thirty years to do!

The green meadows of Ireland

In the midst of all this it emerges that, from my job with the Italians, it had been months that I had not received anything, despite how little it was, they owed me six months.

So I don't know, but from that song I heard in October or in December when I "awoke", things started to appear, it was like certain details showed up that helped me get closest to achieve what I wanted. It happens that one day they told me that they were going to pay me for the six months together, which was a lot of money for me, and at the same time the sales began to grow in the business. That meant I ended up in the span of two months getting the money for the ticket (which was not cheap at all) so I went to the agency and bought the two way ticket: there was no turning back, and I was all set! Of course, for Mom it was like crazy, but, well, she always accompanied me in my crazy things and I looked so excited and happy that she didn't say anything, and for the others, nobody knew yet.

I already had the ticket to go to the concert, the plane ticket, and I was already putting together the itinerary. Of course that mine was very austere, go to hostels because obviously I didn't have enough money to pay a hotel, so I was looking for the cheapest hostels in London, wherever it was... the concert not was there, was to 400 kilometers away from London, so I had to find a hostel in London and in the place of the concert and then return, and as I had decided to set up the trip to Ireland as well, the same, I was looking hostels in Ireland and the flight to get there, anyway it was a bit cheaper because it involved internal flights .

So I put all that together by myself, and at that time I received an email from the band's violinist, Barry. When I see that email I wanted to die, I say: "the violinist wrote to me!", And he told me that it caught his attention that I wrote "greetings from Argentina", well, he began to read and was excited, let's say by the idea of what I told him, what happened to me when I listened to his violin and everything that it generated, even the fact of me making this trip; then, he told me that I was going to be very welcome, of course, and that they were going to play the song in question, Sebastian, and that there was going to be a live choir with 80 vocalists accompanying, so it was going to be an incredible night and that I was going to enjoy it very much.

The Facebook group continued to grow, at that time we were already 24 members, and one of the girls in the group asked me which airport I was leaving from and how I would get there, and I asked her from which airport she was leaving to go to Ireland and she tells me : "I 'll take you! From here the concert is on, I'll take you to the airport because we're close". She did not know me at all yet and she was already offering to take me to the airport, it was like everything, and I mean everything, was lining up so that my trip was perfect. They were all things for the better, it was an incredible energy that had been generated, a beautiful energy, I had come back to life, what's more, they told me that I looked prettier, I had like blossomed, really came back to life! Yes, that, coming back to life, that was what had happened to me…

I already had everything! I bought a suitcase (because obviously I didn't have one), renewed my passport, so everything was ready!

Chapter 6

My first big trip

Imagine my excitement and what it was like to be ready to do that trip, all the adrenaline, everything I had in my head, I felt was going to explode at any moment.

It was my first plane trip, my first trip to another country, and most importantly, this trip was so special for me because it was going to fulfill the dream of my life! So truly everything was set, the suitcase ready and obviously the nerves typical of a first trip, what to do? What are they going to ask me at the airport? What are they going to tell me? Where would I have to go from where my flight would leave? All of that was terrible! I was helped by my cousin, he has always traveled a lot, he told me... "Well, once you pass the customs, you sit in the waiting room, in the gate your flight leaves from and you're ready from there". So I had my family through the phone, obviously, until I took a seat on the plane, and I remember I had a very good travel partner, a quiet one. I imagined the plane, I don't know, the space was so tight where you sat that I thought: "Wow! In the end we travel better by bus!" But you had so much expectation and suddenly you saw everything so reduced. I had chosen a window, I always liked the window since I was a child, and in this case it was like feeling "cornered". I usually have claustrophobia, and then it was like I had to make a plan to not feel like I was drowning, the ceiling was too low, the window was on top of me, the other seat on top of me as well... It was also an issue. So, I was there taking breaths, trying to think of something else, in what the trip would be like, how the concert would be like, until I saw the flight attendant locked the door and there was no turning back...

The takeoff was what felt the most strange in my stomach, like butterflies, but it was beautiful. In fact, today it's the part I like the most about the flight, that sensation you feel in your stomach when taking off, but at that moment it was terrible, it was all new, so that was the start of my great trip.

I arrived at Gatwick, from there I took the train to Victoria Station, which is one of the major ones in London, and the picture is there; in fact, it's the cover of this book, and I asked someone to take the photo for me because the truth was that you had to capture that incredible moment of finally being in London; in the trip of the train, I was nervous and fascinated because I was listening to people speaking in perfect English and looked out the window seeing the typical English styled houses peek out and already some red cabins, and more coming into the city, the famous red double-decker buses also red.

They had told me that I could take a bus from the station to the hostel, but I wanted to give myself the pleasure of taking one of those typical London taxis, old style black, beautiful, that we have seen all our lives in movies and photos. So I gave myself "the luxury" to take a taxi of those and I got an English taxi driver, an elderly man, very polite, who every time we passed by the main attractions (I was already seeing Big Ben, the bridge, and not could believe what my eyes saw!), what I had seen so many times in pictures and movies, he was doing a kind of guided tour and every now and the he hummed a tune, which is very common to listen in Londoners. And I loved those things!

I had no notion of the value of money at the time and I left him 5 pounds as a tip, and, of course, very grateful, she says with his charming accent London: "Oh, many thanks, Madame!" Of course! Obviously, after one already lives here, five pounds is a lot of money, but at that moment I was so happy to be there that all I wanted was to arrive, drop things off and go out, yes, go out and explore London!

So I did that, I got to the hostel, I checked in, after so many hours of travel I obviously took a shower, got dressed and went out, now, I wanted to go through everything! Also, the hostel was close to the main attractions, so I went walking. I also took a tour to do another type of visit to the most touristic places. On the bus, these double-decker specials for tours, just as I was freshly bathed I went upstairs, that day was very cold, there was a lot of wind and the truth is that later, two or three days later, I felt it... that cold affected me. But I was so happy that nothing mattered to me!

I went through everything from the first moment, having everything there so close, and at the same time I saw it and it was hard for me to believe that for example I had "my beloved Big Ben" in front of me as I had dreamed so many times! And I saw the tower of the church clock in my hometown, and I always imagined that at some point it would be the Big Ben, but never thought I'd see it there in front of me... in front... there it was one thing you could not understand, I was not in my head, I didn't quite realize that I was really there!

That day I walked a lot, I went to eat the traditional fish and chips and then, in the afternoon, I had the pleasure of having the typical "six o'clock tea" nothing more and nothing less than in the cafe of the historic Royal Hotel, of 150 years; everything fascinated me, for me it was all beautiful, the people, the way they dressed... I remember that from the bus I saw a man passing by so well-dressed, with braces, with a vest, with a bearing, and he went as if was nothing, just the day to day; and then seeing in a corner, later in the after hour, a group of office workers, all in suits, and the way they stood, that caught my attention because next to them there was a poster with an advertisement of a model, and they were prettier and more elegant, with their particular way of standing and they were just chatting among friends, they were better looking than the model that was in the advertisement! It was funny to see that contrast. Later, for example, a girl came by, dressed all in tulle! Wow, crazy, I thought! And, well, she was happy like that, no one was struck by it, she was wearing a bonnet, I remember, that's what London has, that contrast of styles... it's a cosmopolitan city, right? The truth is that my arrival was incredible.

After that, I went to the Museum of Sherlock Holmes, which I adore! And also I was astonished by it, because every room that you go through is a setting in scene of the different stories emerged to from this fictional character, as in the case of "The Hound of the Baskervilles"; on the second floor you will be visiting the bedroom of the Dr. Watson and Mrs. Hudson's room. Scenes from Sherlock Holmes stories with wax models are displayed on the third floor. Something to note is that it helps to see them as part of the house. Everything looks incredibly real! I did the tour obviously, and then, in the shop, saw all the things that you can take to your house and the museum itself, imagine every moment that we have seen in movies or if you have read the books, I don't know, his pipe, his pen everything, it's like you said "He was here!", or at least that feeling is what you get when you see his personal belongings.

Everything I saw while touring London was incredible. Imagine, fulfilling a dream of practically thirty years... yes, thirty years! Honestly priceless, that is, if you thought about the money that the entire trip had cost (and I already told you that I did it with a very austere criterion) but it was really worth the effort and time that I had waited.

The oddest thing was that I did not know (I was wrong not to hear) was that I arrived just the day of the birthday of the Queen, and at the moment she passed and greeted from his car or hearse and the procession that accompanied her, I was in the hostel bathing; I found out later, I didn't know, and it was incredible because I couldn't believe I had chosen that exact date to travel. The most exciting thing was that it felt like it was a kind of a "welcome" if you will, that was incredible. The same thing happened to me in Ireland: when I arrived in Ireland two days later -I didn't even know- there was a parade and all the streets were closed with security operations and a helicopter flying over Dublin, and it was all due to the 100th anniversary! Of the independence! So everything really coincided with my arrival, on the Queen's birthday and in Ireland on such a significant date for them And I thought that all that could not be just a coincidence, that is, they were dates that appeared because of something in my head when choosing those specific days to travel, obviously without knowing it.

Six o'clock tea in the cafe of the Royal Hotel

At 221B Baker St. Sherlock Holmes Museum

And as already I was mentioned before, I used to say: "I don't want to die without first knowing the green meadows of Ireland". Obviously, I took the plane, I got to Dublin, but to go to the cliffs I had to go to Cork County, and to the southeast. So I asked what was better, more economical or faster, whatever. They told me that the fastest way was the train but it was more expensive, but if I took a bus I'd arrived perfectly fine. So I took a bus that, I remember, the guard was somewhat impatient because the bus in question was-delayed... 3 minutes! As you can see, they are so punctual and don't know the Argentinian lateness! There were four hours of traveling and still two to go and I had begun to feel ill, my temperature was rising. And I thought, with the delirium caused by the fever: "it's good that I always said that I didn't want to die without knowing Ireland, but at least let me get there!"

So I arrived made a mess, I went to the hostel I had booked -which was far away, because the city of Cork has an old part and a new part, in the old one was where the hostel was and the famous Shannon bell tower were located-, and by the way, it was quite far to go to the area with the pubs, business and others. I took a bath and left as I was, fever and all, and I said, "this is not going to spoil my arrival! I'm going to go out anyways!" And the truth was I was more ready to go to bed than to go out, I had nothing left in the tank, actually I was very lethargic, and I remember I went into a pub (it would be seven in the evening and I had no idea about time schedules for food in there), I remember perfectly that I ordered an Irish coffee, because I wanted to try the real one! And the bar tender asks me: "what do you want to accompany it with?" To which I respond with total naturalness: "bring me something sweet". And the man looks at me in amazement and asks me as if to say: "Are you sure you want that?" And in fact he says: "Something sweet with the coffee? Wouldn't you prefer a pork plate with I don't know what...", and he offered me several options that for me it was unthinkable to consume -at that time- with coffee. It turns out that for them it was something very strange to order something sweet with a coffee at seven in the afternoon, which is dinner time for them, even the kitchen of all the places to eat closes at 8 pm. So they offered me, not yet convinced of the craziness that I was about to make, an apple crumble with ice cream, it was very good, and when I tried the Irish coffee, which was with real Irish whiskey (not like the one we were used to ordering with my friends when we went out for a drink in Tandil), I remember I was drinking the first sip and passing by my throat was like a fire that I felt, and believe me that in five minutes I was perfectly fine! I even got over my fever, my decay, everything! It was very funny. And now really nothing could stop me! From there I went to a big pub where there was live music and typical dance, it was beautiful! I also ate a typical Irish meal, so the experience was barbaric, but it was funny to arrive with such a fever and with the Irish whiskey I was over it right away!

My "curious" request for Irish schedules!

The next day I did a tour to the Cliff of Moher, which was not close at all, it was several hours of travel, and when we arrived… it was finally there! In those cliffs that I had seen so much in that meditation, in that kind of visualization that I had while meditating, and feeling that fresh and pure breeze on my face, it was a very windy day too and it was incredible. I could see the tiny rocks in the distance and when we made the water tour later, they were huge! Everything was so beautiful!

If you like, you can enjoy the water tour I took at Cliff of Moher

The next day I went to tour the so-called Ring of Kerry, which was the prairie area; it was incredibly beautiful, it really is an incomparable green. There is the Irish green and you see the grass in England and that is the English green (it is really very funny) and it is not the same one we have in Argentina either. Really when you choose the paint color between Irish green and English green, it's just like that, it's that color.

To get to the lighthouse we saw in my visualization during meditation I had to do research, and it turned out to be the one in Valentia Island; for that reason I settled for three days in Cork, because I was in that area. But to get there I had to travel three hours by bus, then take a ferry to get to the island, take another bus, and it is a small town and I don't know if I had a place to stay, I don't know if I had a ferry to get back there. One day -when I asked, they couldn't tell me with certainty- it was too much travel to be done, and I couldn't get to the point of seeing the lighthouse, of having it in front of me.

The most curious thing was that, on my return from Ireland to London, on the flight I was again sitting near the window and from there I saw that something shining a lot below (imagine when you see the surface of the ground, that the plane starts gaining height) and when I looked more closely... it was the lighthouse of the Valentia Island! I couldn't believe it! It was that lighthouse that seemed to tell me: "Here I am, you are seeing me! You traveled here and managed to see me!" The emotion that I felt was immense because I was sad and disappointed for not having been able to fulfill my own promise to see the lighthouse, but when I saw that image from the window, the feeling of seeing it down there, so small, and that light that shone brightly, the reflection of the crystals where it transmits its light was something incredible! More than a sign! I received many signals on this trip, before and after, everything was telling me: "you are accompanied, your guides are with you, we are taking you to the place where you were at some point, but you do not remember."

Ireland was very exciting, I really enjoyed getting to know those beautiful places and touring them and it was beautiful, it was what I brought back, it was a feeling of having left something there, a burden, let's say like liberation. It was like having reunited with my own soul there and came back accompanied by my soul, merged again in my current body. It was a sensation in my chest of joy and peace, especially peace, for having rediscovered that one, I don't know whether to call her Florencia, that person that I was in another life, that I knew had been there, and that was what completed me. With that feeling and that sensation I came back, with an incredible energy that I found there. Today, when at work or by whatever situation I feel myself with no energy, I feel the need to go there... I say "I need Ireland", and in fact, last year I was having a really bad time on a very ugly job I had previous to the current one, I asked for a few days of vacation and I went to Ireland, and that weekend I was there I recharged myself with its energy and came back with my batteries charged. I don't know well what it is, but it is there something magical about how it feels if you connect with nature. I would not live in Ireland, I would not choose it to settle permanently there, at least not now, because my place is and always will be England, but there is something in Ireland that attracts me, something I need, its air, its people, its aromas, I need that every so often and when I can I do it and I go. Now I would need it but we cannot travel because of the pandemic...

So this trip was amazing, and when I returned to London, I found in the headlines that Prince had just died, and I thought one more thing more! There were so many strong things that had happened, many hard news during my trip, so it was something too weird to digest. And this time I changed to another hostel that was closer to downtown and did other types of tours different from the ones I did with the first one.

I went to Notting Hill and Portobello Road, walked its streets with beautiful houses painted in pastel colors and the endless fair in the middle of the street offering all kinds of objects, specially porcelain! Then, I visited other places like Oxford Street, Piccadilly Circus and Trafalgar Square, among others. But without a doubt, the one that I loved doing the most and that I suggest to all who visit England if they haven't already is Stonehenge! It is a prehistoric monument formed by natural stones positioned in a curious way that give off, when observing them and learning about their history in the museum, an indescribable energy and curiosity. I insist! You have to see it!

All this I went through in only two days because my trip was a 10 day round trip, that is, including the days the flights of 13 hours each, so that was very fleeting, I had it structured in such a way, before traveling, which was to never stop, and when I returned home I was very tired, because it had been a lot going there, taking this train, taking this plane, taking this other train, going to this hostel... Everything was so, so specific in how it was setup but it was perfect, and to this day, I do not know how I made this trip alone, say, my first trip, how I came to take trains, take the same aircraft, all with that emotional and adrenaline baggage as I say I had. And everything turned out to be so perfect, so good, that it was simply that, letting it flow and letting myself be accompanied by my guides, as I say, and enjoying, enjoying that moment, that trip. There will always be that of my first trip, no matter how much I have done others after, but that will always be "my first big trip"!

Cliff of Moher, Irlanda

Caressing the green meadows of Ireland

At Stonehenge Wiltshire, England

Chapter 7

Fulfilling my dream at last

I had come to London, I had traveled, and the anxiety of the first day was gone, still there were many emotions to live, but the most important moment for me was approaching, that was to go to the concert of Steve Harley and Cockney Rebel, the band that had somehow brought me with their song to fulfill my great dream of traveling to London.

As I told you, the concert was not in London, and I had to travel three hours by train because it was in Hull, further north. Another sign was that when I officially moved to England, I happened to go live in London and then in Wimbledon seven months in Doncaster, Yorkshire, and you know what? That's next to Hull! It was something incredible, because it had taken me a long time to get there on the day of the concert and then live one step away, just a few minutes by bus!

Going back to that, it was the same as the second trip that I had go to Croydon to find out all about the papers I needed to come to live here, and find myself getting a ticket -wrongly- to Wimbledon, and I say: "Wimbledon? What am I going to go to do there? Well, I could go see… there are the tennis courts". I admit that tennis never attracted much attention to me, but I decided not to go and get a new ticket that would leave me close to where I was staying. And the next year my first job and place to live for two months was Wimbledon! In other words, there were many signs, as I have already mentioned in previous chapters, in these trips, in the previous one and afterwards.

But let's go back to the big day, April 23, that great night in Hull. I was going to meet, imagine, everyone, or at least most of the people who were in that group that I had created on Facebook, who did not know me personally but they followed me. Besides, seeing the band live, of course! In fact, it was my first live concert because I had never been to a concert, yes I had gone to see artists play, but not with the anticipation of getting a ticket, going to a place and listen to a playing band, I had never done that.

Things were not so good when I arrived in Hull... The city was all cut off because they were undergoing repairs, you couldn't travel much (there were still five hours to go before the concert). I went to the Bed & Breakfast that I had booked (because I did not want a hostel there, I wanted a room for myself), to be calm, change my clothes and put on makeup in my own pace, I did not want to have someone around or from a bunk bed watching me.

When I arrived it was raining; anyways, I had taken, -like a true local- my Londoner umbrella I had bought the first day. I found out that the Bed & Breakfast was closed, no one would answer the door, I rang the bell, knocked, nothing, no one answered. Outside, there were some women talking with a different accent, as I mentioned, they have different accents here in England, and then they spoke to me like that, let's say with an aggressive tone, but in reality it was their way of speaking, it was not that they treated me badly, and then they told me : "don't go, you have to insist because she has an obligation to answer to you"; well, well, they knew the owner of the place because obviously they were neighbors. I grabbed my bag and took the direction towards the city, but you could see it was far from where I was, and that apparently was very close to the stadium of soccer that could be heard, by now, fans cheering on, the unison cry of goooooooaal! or complaining when they missed a shot to the net, the language of football can be understood perfectly regardless of the country! I waited for a taxi that never came, I waited for the bus whose stop I had in front of where I was but never came either, so I decided to go back to the place where I was supposed to stay and insisted and, a few moments later the door finally gets answered. The lovely woman welcomed me very kindly, and accompanied me to what would be my room on the top floor, it was perfect, and it was only one night that I would sleep there –if I could do so– after the concert.

Well, now I had to get ready! It was so hot and I was so sweaty (although I had taken a bath), and I just could not calm myself, I was very anxious, very nervous, just imagine, meeting Steve, I was fascinated with him, admired him deeply. It was like going back in time to those emotions and sensations that one feels as a teenager. So I wanted to look good, I wanted to be perfect and I didn't even know if I could get to know them, I am referring to greeting them. I sort of sensed that perhaps the meeting with some members of the band could take place, because Jackie had told me that they liked it when their fans waited for them to greet them, but it was difficult, I didn't know how I was going to do it.

I asked for a cab and it drove me to the place where the concert was going to be. There were still two hours, Jackie had sent me a message that she was going to be in a pub with other members of the group, but I never found them. I sent a lot of messages, but they didn't answer me, I had gotten sick because I thought that since I had arrived in that city everything was going wrong, as if fate is determined that the perfect day for me would turn into the worst.

So... I walked around as much as I could, because let me say, the streets were all broken with debris and fenced out, so I saw that there is a mall near where the venue of the event was and decided to go to spend time and, incidentally, I would have a coffee.

But time passed and no one came to take my order, I waited for more than ten minutes and no one came, when I got up to leave one of the employees asked me if I needed anything, and I explained that I had been waiting for a long time and no one came had even asked what I wanted, so he apologized, and asked me to sit down again and immediately brought me the coffee I asked for. It was like everything got complicated, and the anxiety I had didn't help much, and it made me feel worse.

Well, finally it was time to enter the concert. I had my ticket, ahead of everyone in the row to be the first to enter the venue. The person who received us, also a very typical English man and very attentive, said to me "where do you come from?" And when I said "from Argentina", he was very surprised and asked me if I came exclusively for that event, which I answer that indeed it was. And he couldn't believe that I had made such a journey just to be there, and he makes me go in. And, well, I walked in and sighed, I was finally there! I had reserved my seat and as I remembered the graphic when I bought it, it should be in the second row, so I went to that place and I could not find it and the person who helped with the locations told me: "no, no, no, you are here", He goes back, back, back and I say: "no, stop, I'm on the second row", and he says: "no, you're not second row, you're on row 11"(I think it was). And I realized what happened ... I had seen the diagram of the place with the stage and the seats, and when selecting my seat, obviously I did it the other way around, I selected the second row, but starting from the back. As I already mentioned, it was the first time I bought a ticket online.

Well, there I was already devastated, I started to cry because it was between the emotion that I had, the nerves, and everything had been going so badly, I said "no, everything can't turn out like this, this can't be happening!"

Already resigned I took my seat and, since they saw that I was uneasy, they asked me what was happening to me, and then I told them that I had made that trip just to be here and now I had a seat so far from the stage. There, they introduced themselves and I met some of the people who later, or rather, after that day, joined the group. All were very friendly people, trying to comfort me, to speak with me and to make me feel better, they said that everything was going to be okay, that I had come so far that now, I should just enjoy. But it was not the same; I wanted to have them there, in front of me. Right there, I saw Jackie coming in, I called her and she recognized me right away, she came over and gave me a hug, obviously, because, of course, we had been communicating through the group for two months, but now meeting in person was different. Then she says to me: "Come with me I'm going to introduce you to the rest", and she introduced me to the others who already were located in the front rows.

Previously, when I was walking through the streets looking for the pub where Jackie and the others would meet, I listened to someone pronounce my name, "Florencia", she called me, and I look and think for a moment: "Who calls me Florencia here?" And this was one of the fans and a member of the Facebook group, Paul, who had recognized me, there was July also waiting the hour of the concert, and on seeing me walk they noticed it was me. The situation was very nice and funny! And well, he was one of the people who were also sitting in the front, very close to the stage, and he was with the other members, some from the group and others not, but they were arriving later.

Then I told them about "my misery" (for me it was all a tragedy) and what had happened since I had come to that city.

As the concert was about to start, I returned to my seat. First, a very good local support band played and, after a while they started to play, I saw Jackie who came looking for me and told me to follow her, she had a surprise for me, and it was that one of them, more precisely, Paul, the one who had met me in the street, gave me his seat. I couldn't believe it and I said: "noooo, you're not going to give me your seat" To which he replies: "yes, yes, it's all yours, you deserve it! I've been watching them live for years, it's fine, it's one more night, so sit here". Very happily I thanked him for his gesture Now everything seemed to settle and began to be all as I had planned: sitting in the second row, and they were there, in front of me. When they came to the stage, woaaaaah, I had seen all their videos and all their gestures as they played each song, the violinist, guitarist, all the gestures that I saw in the video one after another, one after another I had seen and I saw again so many times, that I knew all their gestures and songs by heart! And now they were there, in front of me, performing them, it was something difficult to explain in words, but my heart was beating so hard and I wouldn't stop smiling and singing and I was sitting with other people and they were saying: "she came from Argentina!" And all were left saying, "Wow, from Argentina, and you came just to see this? And I, very proud of my achievement, answered them firmly: "that's right, I traveled thirteen hours just to see them play live because they brought me here", and they looked at me in awe and it was such a story!

They sang several songs and the most anticipated moment of the night arrived and the violinist had already told me by email that they were going to play, and the piano began to sound to start *Sebastian*! This was, in short, the song that had brought me to England to fulfill my dream. The choir of 80 members placed themselves behind the band, at the bottom of the stage, on the steps, and had amazing voices and sang the choir, and the violinist winks at me from above the scene like an accomplice, knowing it was the moment of my favorite part.

I was like floating on a cloud, it was so exciting to listen to it live and everything that had happened after hearing it for the first time that night in October, that I couldn't stop the tears from flowing from my eyes, but this time they were only of happiness. I said, and in fact I said it to the one next to me, "this is the song that brought me here."

And, well, they made an intermediate break and when they returned to the stage, they played a couple more songs, and at one point Steve interrupts and starts talking, and then he says: "tonight is very special, because besides being...", because that night they paid tribute to a musician who had been his great friend and who had died several years ago, in fact, his family was there. There were also musicians who had joined the band and a guitarist of none other than David Bowie! Can you believe that! Steve continued talking, "but it is not the only reason this is special, but because I have been told that there is someone..." and then by my side I had who I'd later know was Jim, and he starts nudging me and telling me: "it's you! It's you! And I said "no way, He is not talking about me!", and while Steve was still talking: "...someone who traveled a lot, a lot of kilometers to be here today and come to see me", he would say and joke about it"... who came from Argentina just to see me", and Jim nudged me by my side: "see! it was you, it was you! ". And then Steve uses his hands as a visor for the lights he had in front and asks: "Where is Florencia?" And they all pointed to me: "Here she is! Here she is!" And he invites me to get up and tells me: "come here, come here", I was ashamed, I don't know, I didn't know what to say or what to do. And he makes me go on stage. I should mention at this point that I wanted a book from him that I had been ordering about a month before my trip and it was out of stock and there was no way to get it. And to my surprise he tells me: "I have something for you, it's my book." I wanted to die, my excitement was so great because I had wished for that book and wanted that book so much! And there himself, in front of everyone, puts a dedication and gives me an autograph, and I at this moment turn and look to the public, and they were all clapping and cheering and I said to myself: "Wow, the audience of a British band applauding me? A girl who comes from Argentina and nobody knows". It was an instant eternal enough for me, as well as a still image of that moment of the audience clapping and shouting and cheering, and it was something incomparable, inexplicable, that the memory of my retina will keep until my last day.

Think about what I told you before, about everything that had been going poorly and roughly before the concert, now it had become what I had imagined for that night, when everything was perfect, and the emotion and joy didn't fit on my chest. So, well, he finishes writing and hands me the book, I am very happy, very excited, obviously very grateful, I returned to my seat and continue the concert. When it finished, we went down to the lobby and here comes the most amazing and crazy thing that could have happened: they came all to greet and meet, to see who was the Argentinian that had come to see to the band, who had traveled from so far and for which they had stopped the concert to make mention of it. Then they came to meet me, they took photos with me and that was crazy, because I said "but the band is there", that is, "I am nobody", and among them was a journalist who worked for the BBC in Hull and also me did a kind of brief interview and took a picture with me, and I said "someone from the BBC". I couldn't believe the repercussion that my arrival there and my presence itself had had.

It was a very cold night, I was somewhat unsheltered, so, adding that night, I had already been cold on the tour the first day in London, and that was why, when I traveled to Ireland, it was the next day after the concert, I arrived with that flu-like state and fever (apart from emotions, of course!).

We left and waited for hours outside in the cold, that, let me put it this way, it was one of those where you are trembling and want to talk but you bit yourself because you're shivering, well, like that! But it was all so beautiful, such an intense night that I did not care about anything. And there was Deborah, which today is one of my best friends and lives very close to my city, Jackie, of course, who is also, and Paul, we were with them and some few more waiting to see if Steve or one of the members of the band would come out. At one point, a man who was also waiting with another friend came, and he extended his hand and congratulated me not only for what Steve had said about me, but because "I had beat them" on distance traveled to see them, since they were from the United States.

Little by little the musicians started to appear and they came to me to meet and greet me and I told them, "but you're in the band! How are you going to come to say hello to me?" And they responded very kindly "but it's what you did, is very admirable, it is worth greet and congratulate you." So they were happy to take photos with me. I do not know if I'll ever be in a situation comparable to that night, but even if I do, what I lived that day, I will never forget it!

I took pictures with all of them, with other fans and we kept waiting and waiting and, well... we already assumed that we were leaving without seeing Steve because it was already late; in that I saw in the middle of a group of the people and no one had seen him, there was Steve! I told the others: "It's Steve", and he was there and nobody saw him or heard me, and they were all talking on their own, and I called him out loud: "Steve!" He turns and I call him again "Steve!" And he sees me and opens his arms and says – in his own way-

"Florencia"! (I always get emotional when I remember it), and he gives me such an incredible, tender, passionate hug, one could say, if the term fits, and practically lifts me up, and I thought to myself: "I can't believe I'm hugging the person I had seen so many times in the last two months in all his videos!" I had dreamed of that meeting so many times, that it would be like this, as beautiful as it was, and he gives me a kiss on both cheeks and he turned to embrace me another time, and it was so much the joy that this man had as well because he, in some way, also went back in time, to those times where fans wrote to him and waited at the exit of the concerts, and I might have reminded him of everything and that was why his reaction was so charming. The funny thing was to see in his eyes the expression of his look, the joy he had for knowing me, and it was almost the same as mine for knowing him.

I had brought a book for him from Argentina as a gift, with landscapes and descriptions of the country, very nice, translated into both languages (English and Spanish), and he was very moved when I gave it to him because he really did not expect it and he said: "Have you brought me a gift?", And I replied: "yes, of course, I brought it for you, somehow I wanted to thank you because today I am here thanks to you and your music", and inside that book I put the letter with everything that I said in another chapter, where I tell all the process I went through since I heard the song; until I came to London and then, to the meeting in the concert. When I gave him the book, I indicated that inside the book there was a letter for him with which he would understand much better what I meant by saying that I owed him that I was there, and he hugged me again so tightly and with so much emotion, and It was an unforgettable moment because it is in those moments when you feel that the other is really happy to see you and meet you.

After that, he continued greeting to fans, talking to some of them, and the girls came to ask me how the meeting had been, so I told them, and truly it had really gotten late. My friends were all in the same hotel downtown and I was the only one who was alone in another place further away, so Paul with the others took me in the car and there we said goodbye, and obviously I thanked them again for so much kindness, Jackie would see us next day because she would pick me up to take me to the airport in Doncaster (who would think that night that, years later, I would live for seven months in that place!). When I got to the B&B and I went to my room… how you can think that was I going to sleep! I wouldn't get a wink of sleep with all those images in my head! It was impossible! I did not know what to do, whom to tell, whom to talk about this with, I wanted to shout out of joy, but I could not because everyone was asleep, it was past midnight. And then I remember that in my country it was still early, so I sent a message to my brother who had WhatsApp (my mother at that time did not have her cell phone, I later bought her one so that we could communicate before coming in my second trip), I told him everything that had happened in great detail, and he answered my text messages and called my mother on the landline and was telling her what I said, and they couldn't believe it either, Because the truth was that everything had been so incredible and moving that it seemed that I was dreaming, but no, I was more than awake fulfilling what had been my great dream.

I couldn't sleep that night and the following morning Jackie was there with her car, waiting to go to the airport where the great adventure to know Ireland would come, but I already told you about that in the previous chapter.

Ticket I received in the mail before I knew if I could travel

Thanking Steve Harley, after giving me and signing his book on stage

Acknowledgements

- ALEJANDRO DAMIAN GATTI RICCETTI, Tandil, Buenos Aires, Argentina

- ANITA UBEROI – NRK, Oslo, Noruega

- CHAMALÚ, Bolivia

- GABRIELA INES LARA – FM del Sol, Benito Juárez, Buenos Aires, Argentina

- JIMENA BARRIONUEVO – Bienestar LN (Diario La Nación) Buenos Aires, Argentina

- JOSÉ CANTERO – Diario El Fénix, Benito Juárez, Buenos Aires, Argentina

- LINA DE AMICIS – WORKANA

- MAITE AYALA - WORKANA

- SANTIAGO ALEGRE – WORKANA

- YENNY MEDINA - WORKANA

- STEVE HARLEY through RACHEL CAMERON –Comeuppance, Sudbury, Suffolk, UK

- TRIXIE MOURA, La Paloma, Rocha, Uruguay

- And of course, my deepest gratitude to my teacher FRANCISCO NAVARRO LARA, because without his teachings, this book would still be only in my head.

Woburn abbey

Photo by Deborah Rollings

Contact links with Florencia Menna

Website:

www.florenciamennacoach.com

Instagram:

https://www.instagram.com/floraromadeflor/

Facebook:

(1) Florencia Menna - Personal Coach | Facebook

E-mail:

floraromadeflor@gmail.com

Twitter:

http://twitter.com/floraroma

YouTube:

Florencia Menna - YouTube

LinkedIn:

(2) Florencia Menna | LinkedIn

Make your dream come true!

August 13th, 2020

www.ingramcontent.com/pod-product-compliance
Lightning Source LLC
Chambersburg PA
CBHW041552120626
46551CB00002B/175